W9-CLZ-533

herman melville

MOBY DICK

adapted by

bill SIENKIEWICZ

artist

bill sienkiewicz
and dan chichester
writers

willie schubert
letterer

BERKLEY/FIRST PUBLISHING

The sea fascinated and preoccupied Herman Melville, and figured in most of his writing. **Moby Dick**, Melville's most famous work, represented the peak of his literary attempt to convey in words the sweep, majesty, power and peril of the oceans. By the time Melville began work on **Moby Dick,** he had achieved fame for two romantic novels, *Typee* and *Omoo,* and several stories. Published in 1851, the novel was dedicated to Nathaniel Hawthorne, a friend whom Melville saw frequently while writing his epic novel. **Moby Dick** was a literary triumph for Melville, but his popularity declined in later years, following the publication of several less-successful works. At the time of his death in 1891, he was regarded as a minor author. In the early 1920s, a critical rediscovery and reappraisal restored his reputation as a major American literary figure, an early master of symbolic yet realistic narrative, rythmic prose and social criticism. Generally considered a novel, **Moby Dick** is also an exhaustive compilation of painstakingly researched material about whales and the whaling industry of the 19th century. Of the book's 143 chapters, more than 40 are devoted exclusively to factual discourses on the business and life of whaling. Principally for this reason, **Moby Dick** is renowned for its sense of time and place — its ability to summon up a way of life long past. It is remarkable for its broad appeal: some readers are excited by the seafaring adventure story; some are enraptured by the psychological study of obsessive madness; and others are absorbed by the deep and penetrating symbolic allegory of the disaster that awaits when man tries to constitute himself as a god, when man becomes evil to fight evil.

Moby Dick
Classics Illustrated, Number 4

Wade Roberts, Editorial Director
Alex Wald, Art Director

PRINTING HISTORY
1st edition published February 1990

Copyright © 1990 by The Berkley Publishing Group and First Publishing, Inc. All rights reserved.No part of this book may be reproduced or transmitted in any form or by any means, electronic or mechanical, including photocopying, recording, or by information storage and retrieval system, without express written permission from the publishers.

For information, address: The Berkley Publishing Group, 200 Madison Avenue, New York, New York 10016.

ISBN 0-425-12023-6

TRADEMARK NOTICE: Classics Illustrated® is a registered trademark of Frawley Corporation. The Classics Illustrated logo is a trademark of The Berkley Publishing Group and First Publishing, Inc. "Berkley" and the stylized "B" are trademarks of The Berkley Publishing Group. "First Publishing" and the stylized "1F" are trademarks of First Publishing, Inc.

Distributed by Berkley Sales & Marketing, a division of The Berkley Publishing Group, 200 Madison Avenue, New York, New York 10016.

Printed in the United States of America
1 2 3 4 5 6 7 8 9 0

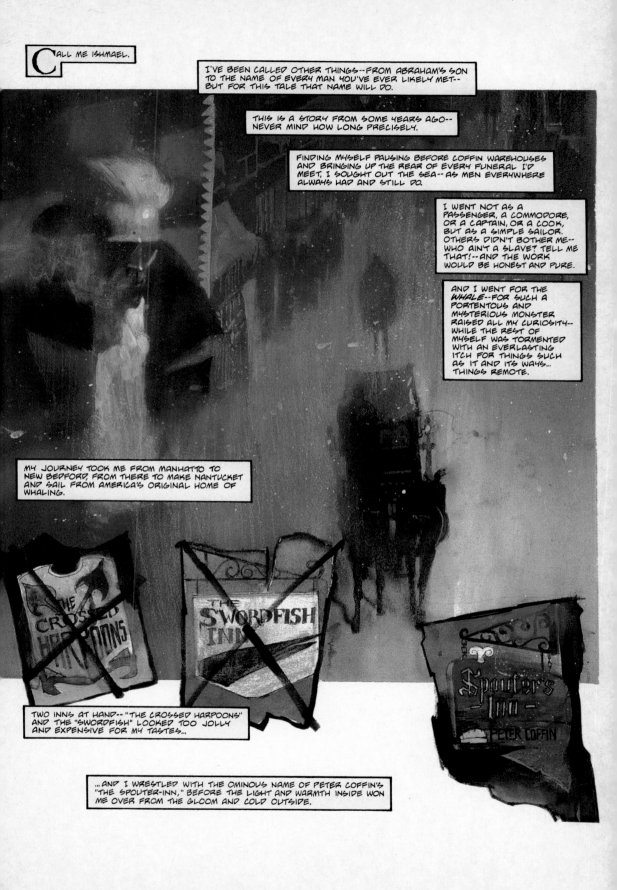

CALL ME ISHMAEL.

I'VE BEEN CALLED OTHER THINGS--FROM ABRAHAM'S SON TO THE NAME OF EVERY MAN YOU'VE EVER LIKELY MET-- BUT FOR THIS TALE THAT NAME WILL DO.

THIS IS A STORY FROM SOME YEARS AGO-- NEVER MIND HOW LONG PRECISELY.

FINDING MYSELF PAUSING BEFORE COFFIN WAREHOUSES AND BRINGING UP THE REAR OF EVERY FUNERAL I'D MEET, I SOUGHT OUT THE SEA-- AS MEN EVERYWHERE ALWAYS HAD AND STILL DO.

I WENT NOT AS A PASSENGER, A COMMODORE, OR A CAPTAIN, OR A COOK, BUT AS A SIMPLE SAILOR. OTHERS DIDN'T BOTHER ME-- WHO AIN'T A SLAVE? TELL ME THAT!--AND THE WORK WOULD BE HONEST AND PURE.

AND I WENT FOR THE *WHALE*--FOR SUCH A PORTENTOUS AND MYSTERIOUS MONSTER RAISED ALL MY CURIOSITY-- WHILE THE REST OF MYSELF WAS TORMENTED WITH AN EVERLASTING ITCH FOR THINGS SUCH AS IT AND ITS WAYS... THINGS REMOTE.

MY JOURNEY TOOK ME FROM MANHATTO TO NEW BEDFORD, FROM THERE TO MAKE NANTUCKET AND SAIL FROM AMERICA'S ORIGINAL HOME OF WHALING.

TWO INNS AT HAND-- "THE CROSSED HARPOONS" AND THE "SWORDFISH" LOOKED TOO JOLLY AND EXPENSIVE FOR MY TASTES...

...AND I WRESTLED WITH THE OMINOUS NAME OF PETER COFFIN'S "THE SPOUTER-INN," BEFORE THE LIGHT AND WARMTH INSIDE WON ME OVER FROM THE GLOOM AND COLD OUTSIDE.

IT WAS SO LOW AND DARK IN THE SPOUTER I WAS REMINDED OF BEING INSIDE A CONDEMNED SHIP.

THE PAINTING ON THE WALL DID NOTHING TO LIGHTEN THE MOOD-- IT WAS A BOGGY, SOGGY, SQUITCHY PICTURE, TRULY ENOUGH TO DRIVE A NERVOUS MAN DISTRACTED.

BUT THE WHALERS THERE THAT NIGHT WERE CONCERNED ONLY WITH GETTING TO THE BAR AT THE BACK OF THE INN--

--PASSING THROUGH AN ARCHWAY MADE OF A JAWBONE OF A WHALE, THOSE JAWS OF SWIFT DESTRUCTION...

I WAS TOLD I WOULD BE SHARING A BED WITH A HARPOONER...

...AS IT WOULD NO DOUBT BE LATE BY THE TIME THE HARPOONER RETURNED--

...A SOUTH SEAS SAVAGE BY THE NAME OF QUEEQUEG.

MISTER COFFIN URGED ME TO GO TO BED...

--GIVEN THE FACT THAT HE WAS OUT SELLING HIS COLLECTION OF *HUMAN HEADS.*

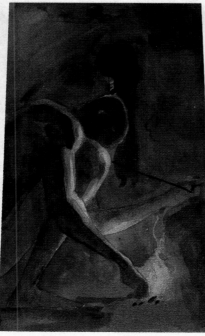

SOON MY PRESENCE BECAME KNOWN TO THE HARPOONER.

WHO-E DEBEL YOU? YOU NO SPEAK-E, DAM-ME I KILL-E!

AFTER MISTER COFFIN RUSHED INTO THE ROOM AND ASSURED ME THAT THE CANNIBAL WOULD NOT KILL ME, WE WERE BOTH SATISFIED.

I WAS WILLING TO SHARE HALF OF ANY DECENT MAN'S BLANKET, AND A MAN CAN BE HONEST IN ANY SORT OF SKIN. BETTER TO SLEEP WITH A SOBER CANNIBAL THAN A DRUNKEN CHRISTIAN.

I NEVER SLEPT BETTER IN MY LIFE.

IN THE MORNING, I FOUND QUEEQUEG'S ARM THROWN AROUND ME TIGHTLY... AS THOUGH NAUGHT BUT DEATH SHOULD PART US TWAIN.

AS THE LANDLORD SHOUTED, "GRUB HO!", I WAS TAKEN WITH THE WHALERS--

--OF GREAT COURAGE AND DARING AT SEA-- TAME AND QUIET ON LAND, OUT OF THEIR ELEMENT.

ONLY QUEEQUEG SHOWED NONE OF THIS SHYNESS. HE SPEARED HIS BEEFSTEAK EAGERLY, RELISHING THE RARE MEAT-- HE WAS AFTER ALL, A CANNIBAL.

THE PULPIT IS EVER THE EARTH'S FOREMOST PART-- THE REST COMES IN ITS REAR--THE PULPIT LEADS THE WORLD. YES, THE WORLD'S A SHIP ON ITS PASSAGE OUT, AND NOT A VOYAGE COMPLETE-- AND THE PULPIT IS ITS PROW!

NO FISHERMAN ABOUT TO SAIL THE WORLD'S SEAS WOULD FAIL TO PAY A CALL AT THE WHALEMAN'S CHAPEL.

FATHER MAPPLE HAD TAKEN THAT DAY'S SERMON FROM THE STORY OF JONAH--I WAS NOT ABOUT TO LET THE SIGNIFICANCE OF THAT CHOICE ESCAPE ME...

IF WE OBEY GOD, WE MUST DISOBEY OURSELVES. AND IT IS IN THIS DISOBEYING OURSELVES, WHEREIN THE HARDNESS OF OBEYING GOD CONSISTS!

I OBEYED MY GOD, AND QUEEQUEG, HIS--A PAGAN IDOL HE CALLED YOJO.

I DID NOT MIND JOINING MY NEW FRIEND IN HIS WORSHIP, FOR MY GOD IS MAGNANIMOUS, AND COULD NOT BE JEALOUS OF AN INSIGNIFICANT BIT OF BLACK WOOD.

FURTHER, TO WORSHIP IS TO DO THE WILL OF GOD...AND WHAT IS THE WILL OF GOD?--TO DO TO MY FELLOW MAN WHAT I WOULD HAVE MY FELLOW MAN TO DO TO ME--THAT IS THE WILL OF GOD.

WE SMOKED TOGETHER... WHEN THE SMOKE ENDED, QUEEQUEG PRESSED HIS FOREHEAD TO MINE AND PROCLAIMED US MARRIED--BOSOM FRIENDS WHO WOULD DEFEND EACH OTHER TO THE DEATH.

WE NAPPED AND CHATTED IN BED, OUR BLANKETS MORE WARM AND SNUG BECAUSE OF THE CHILL OF THE ROOM-- FOR TO TRULY ENJOY BODILY WARMTH, SOME SMALL PART OF YOU MUST BE COLD, FOR THERE IS NO QUALITY IN THIS WORLD THAT IS NOT WHAT IT IS MERELY BY CONTRAST. NOTHING EXISTS IN ITSELF.

QUEEQUEG SPOKE OF HIS NATIVE ISLAND, KOKOVO, OF HIS FATHER, THE KING, OF JOINING THE CREW OF A WHALING SHIP TO LEARN MORE ABOUT CHRISTIANITY AND HELPING HIS PEOPLE WITH THE ADVANCED IDEAS OF THAT CIVILIZED RELIGION.

I ASKED HIM WHETHER HE DID NOT PROPOSE GOING BACK, AND HAVING A CORONATION; SINCE HE MIGHT NOW CONSIDER HIS FATHER DEAD AND GONE.

QUEEQUEG ANSWERED, "NO, NOT YET," FEARFUL THAT CHRISTIANS HAD UNFITTED HIM FOR ASCENDING THE PURE AND UNDEFILED THRONE OF THIRTY PAGAN KINGS BEFORE HIM.

BY AND BY HE WOULD RETURN--AS SOON AS HE FELT HIMSELF BAPTIZED ANEW.

NEXT MORNING, WE WENT DOWN TO THE MOSS, THE LITTLE PACKET SCHOONER SET TO TAKE US TO NANTUCKET. ONCE UNDER WAY, ONE OF THE PASSENGERS--A BUMPKIN--WAS CAUGHT MIMICKING QUEEQUEG BEHIND HIS BACK.

I THOUGHT THE BUMPKIN'S HOUR OF DOOM WAS COME, AS THE BRAWNY SAVAGE TOSSED THE FELLOW HIGH IN THE AIR AND LET HIM DROP HEAVY ON THE DEC

AS THE SHIP'S CAPTAIN CAME RUNNING TO THREATEN QUEEQUEG, A BOOM--LOOKING LIKE THE LOWER JAW OF AN EXASPERATED WHALE-- BROKE LOOSE, KNOCKIN THE BUMPKIN OVERBOA

IT WAS QUEEQUEG WHO DOVE INTO THE FREEZING WATER TO RESCUE THE OAF. I VOWED THEN I WOULD NEVER LET MY FRIEND OUT OF MY SIGHT...

...EVEN AS HE DRIED OFF, CASUAL IN HIS HEROISM, AS IF SAYING TO HIMSELF, "IT'S A MUTUAL, JOINT STOCK WORLD...WE CANNIBALS MUST HELP THESE CHRISTIANS."

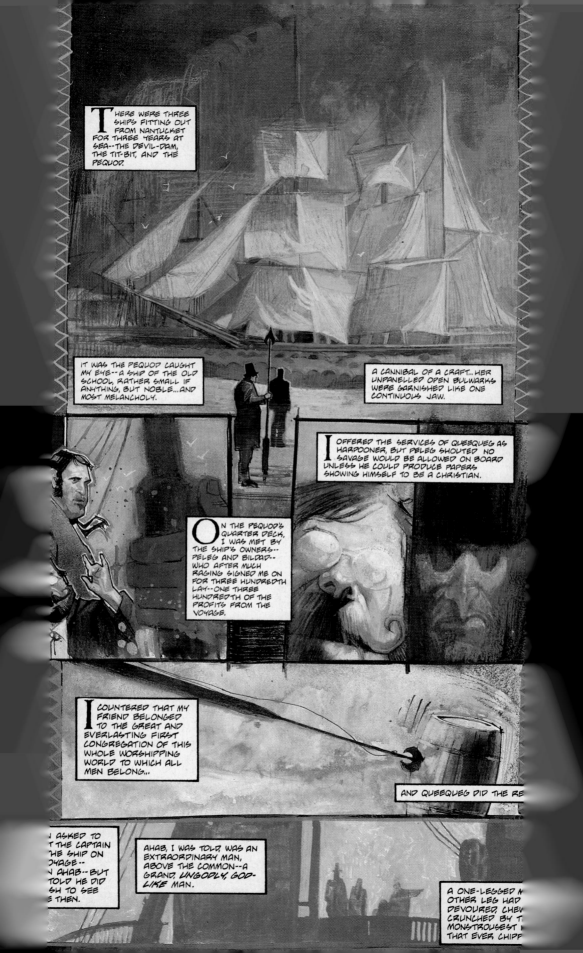

THERE WERE THREE SHIPS FITTING OUT FROM NANTUCKET FOR THREE YEARS AT SEA--THE DEVIL-DAM, THE TIT-BIT, AND THE PEQUOD.

IT WAS THE PEQUOD CAUGHT MY EYE--A SHIP OF THE OLD SCHOOL, RATHER SMALL IF ANYTHING, BUT NOBLE...AND MOST MELANCHOLY.

A CANNIBAL OF A CRAFT... HER UNPANELLED OPEN BULWARKS WERE GARNISHED LIKE ONE CONTINUOUS JAW.

I OFFERED THE SERVICES OF QUEEQUEG AS HARPOONER, BUT PELEG SHOUTED NO SAVAGE WOULD BE ALLOWED ON BOARD UNLESS HE COULD PRODUCE PAPERS SHOWING HIMSELF TO BE A CHRISTIAN.

ON THE PEQUOD'S QUARTER DECK, I WAS MET BY THE SHIP'S OWNERS-- PELEG AND BILDAD-- WHO AFTER MUCH RAGING SIGNED ME ON FOR THREE HUNDREDTH LAY--ONE THREE HUNDREDTH OF THE PROFITS FROM THE VOYAGE.

I COUNTERED THAT MY FRIEND BELONGED TO THE GREAT AND EVERLASTING FIRST CONGREGATION OF THIS WHOLE WORSHIPPING WORLD TO WHICH ALL MEN BELONG...

AND QUEEQUEG DID THE RE

I ASKED TO T THE CAPTAIN HE SHIP ON OYAGE-- N AHAB--BUT TOLD HE DID SH TO SEE E THEN.

AHAB, I WAS TOLD, WAS AN EXTRAORDINARY MAN, ABOVE THE COMMON--A GRAND, UNGODLY, GOD-LIKE MAN.

A ONE-LEGGED N OTHER LEG HAD DEVOURED, CHEW CRUNCHED BY T MONSTROUSEST THAT EVER CHIPP

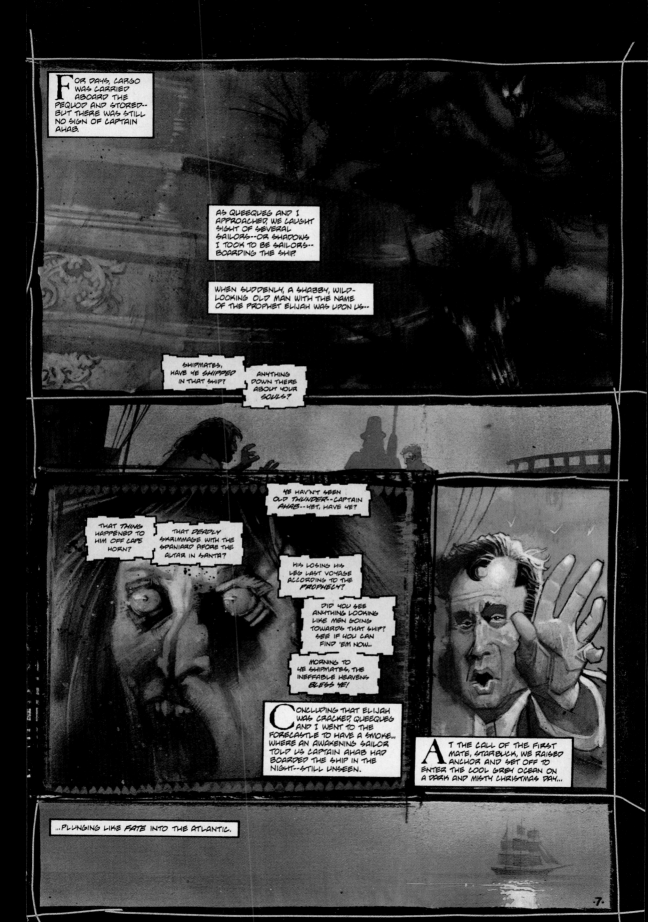

FOR DAYS, CARGO WAS CARRIED ABOARD THE PEQUOD AND STORED-- BUT THERE WAS STILL NO SIGN OF CAPTAIN AHAB.

AS QUEEQUEG AND I APPROACHED, WE CAUGHT SIGHT OF SEVERAL SAILORS--OR SHADOWS I TOOK TO BE SAILORS-- BOARDING THE SHIP.

WHEN SUDDENLY, A SHABBY, WILD- LOOKING OLD MAN WITH THE NAME OF THE PROPHET ELIJAH WAS UPON US--

SHIPMATES, HAVE YE SHIPPED IN THAT SHIP?

ANYTHING DOWN THERE ABOUT YOUR SOULS?

YE HAVN'T SEEN OLD THUNDER--CAPTAIN AHAB--YET, HAVE YE?

THAT THING HAPPENED TO HIM OFF CAPE HORN?

THAT DEADLY SKRIMMAGE WITH THE SPANIARD AFORE THE ALTAR IN SANTA?

HIS LOSING HIS LEG LAST VOYAGE ACCORDING TO THE PROPHECY?

DID YOU SEE ANYTHING LOOKING LIKE MEN GOING TOWARDS THAT SHIP? SEE IF YOU CAN FIND 'EM NOW...

MORNING TO YE SHIPMATES, THE INEFFABLE HEAVENS BLESS YE!

CONCLUDING THAT ELIJAH WAS CRACKED, QUEEQUEG AND I WENT TO THE FORECASTLE TO HAVE A SMOKE... WHERE AN AWAKENING SAILOR TOLD US CAPTAIN AHAB HAD BOARDED THE SHIP IN THE NIGHT--STILL UNSEEN.

AT THE CALL OF THE FIRST MATE, STARBUCK, WE RAISED ANCHOR AND SET OFF TO ENTER THE COOL GREY OCEAN ON A DARK AND MISTY CHRISTMAS DAY...

...PLUNGING LIKE FATE INTO THE ATLANTIC.

SOME WOULD THINK THE VOCATION OF US WHALEMEN IS, AT BEST, A BUTCHERING SORT OF BUSINESS. BUTCHERS WE ARE, THAT IS TRUE. BUT BUTCHERS ALSO HAVE BEEN ALL MARTIAL COMMANDERS WHOM THE WORLD INVARIABLY DELIGHTS TO HONOR.

LOOK AT THIS MATTER IN OTHER LIGHTS; WEIGH IT IN ALL SORTS OF SCALES; SEE WHAT WE WHALEMEN ARE, AND HAVE BEEN:

WHALING HAS BROUGHT GRAND WEALTH TO THE NATIONS OF THE WORLD! MUCH OF THE WORLD'S GREAT EXPLORING HAS BEEN DONE BY THE WHALE SHIPS! THE OIL THAT LIGHTS THE LAMPS YOU READ THIS BY WAS BROUGHT BACK BY WHALEMEN!

JOB WROTE THE FIRST ACCOUNT OF OUR LEVIATHAN IN NO LESS A BOOK THAN THE BIBLE! OUR DIGNITY THE HEAVENS ATTEST WITH THE CONSTELLATION CETUS TO THE SOUTH!

BUT AT THAT TIME, THERE WAS STILL MUCH TO LEARN...

OF THE MYSTERIOUS CAPTAIN AHAB, ALWAYS HIDDEN BEHIND HIS CLOSED DOOR--

--AND HIS MORE VISIBLE MATES AND THEIR HARPOONERS.

WITH QUEEQUEG WAS STARBUCK, A FIRST MATE OF UNAIDED VIRTUE OR RIGHT-MINDEDNESS, A MAN WHO WOULD NOT PERSIST IN FIGHTING A FISH THAT TOO MUCH PERSISTED IN FIGHTING BACK.

IN CONTRAST TO STARBUCK'S COUR-AGE AND BRAVERY WAS THE INVULNERABLE JOLLITY OF INDIFFER-ENCE AND RECKLESS-NESS THAT MARKED THE SECOND MATE, STUBB.

...UNLIKE FLASK, THE THIRD MATE, LIVING IN A WORLD OF PERVADING MEDIOCRITY OF MERELY WAITING TO KILL, WITH NO ROOM FOR REVERENCE FOR THE GIANT FISH HE HUNTED. TO FLASK, THE WONDROUS WHALE WAS BUT A SPECIES OF MAGNIFIED MOUSE.

GOOD-HUMORED, EASY AND CARELESS, HE LIVED FOR THE PLEASURE OF THE HUNT...

THESE SHIP'S KNIGHTS WERE ATTENDED BY THEIR SQUIRES:

STUBB BY TASHTEGO, AN UNMIXED WILD INDIAN, AN INHERITOR OF THE UNVITIATED BLOOD OF THE PROUD WARRIOR HUNTERS WHO CAME BEFORE HIM...

...AND FLASK BY DAGGOO, A GIGANTIC COAL-BLACK NEGRO SAVAGE, RETAINING A CERTAIN BARBARIC VIRTUE IN HIS PRIMITIVE EXISTENCE.

FINALLY, THE MORNING CAME THAT I HAD BEEN WAITING FOR.

THERE, ON THE QUARTER DECK, A MAN MADE OF SOLID BRONZE, BALANCING ATOP A BARBARIC WHITE LEG CARVED OF WHALE BONE...

LOOKING LIKE A MAN CUT AWAY FROM THE STAKE, WHEN FIRE HAS OVERRUNNINGLY *WASTED* ALL THE LIMBS WITHOUT *CONSUMING* THEM...

STANDING THERE ERECT WITH AN INFINITY OF FIRMEST FORTITUDE, A DETERMINATE, UNSURRENDERABLE WILLFULNESS, IN THE FIXED AND FEARLESS, FORWARD DEDICATION OF THAT GLANCE...

...MOODY, STRICKEN AHAB STOOD BEFORE US WITH A CRUCIFIXION IN HIS FACE.

There was to be no rest for the captain, no pleasures.

Tormented by sleeplessness--and perhaps other things--Captain Ahab paced the quarter deck at night, his thumping ivory beating a devil's tattoo over the heads of his weary mates belowdecks.

He tossed the still lighted pipe into the sea. The fire hissed in the waves, dying out along with Ahab's ties to home.

"How now," he soliloquized over his pipe, "this smoking no longer soothes. This thing that is meant for sereneness, to send up mild white vapors among mild white hairs, not among torn iron-grey locks like mine. I'll smoke no more--"

He was now devoted only to the TERRORS of the UNKNOWN SEA--

Ahab was full of riddles, going into the after hold every night; what's that for, I wanted to know... who was it had made appointments with him in the hold?

--AND THE WHITE WHALE he kept a sharp eye for...

THERE WAS A PRIZE OF A SPANISH OUNCE OF GOLD FOR THE MAN WHO WOULD SEE *MOBY DICK* FIRST--THAT GREAT WHITE WHALE WITH A CROOKED JAW AND THREE HOLES IN HIS STARBOARD FLUKE.

IT WAS MOBY DICK HAD DISMASTED AHAB'S LEG, MOBY DICK AHAB NOW SWORE *VENGEANCE* ON...

ONLY STARBUCK WAS NOT TAKEN WITH THE CAPTAIN'S PASSION. "VENGEANCE ON A DUMB BRUTE, THAT SIMPLY SMOTE THEE FROM BLINDEST INSTINCT! *MADNESS!*" HE ARGUED. "TO BE ENRAGED WITH A DUMB THING, CAPTAIN AHAB, SEEMS BLASPHEMOUS."

ONLY STARBUCK DID NOT CLING TO AHAB'S PHILOSOPHY. "ALL VISIBLE OBJECTS, MAN, ARE BUT PASTEBOARD MASKS. IN EACH EVENT, SOME UNKNOWN BUT STILL REASONING THING PUTS FORTH THE MOULDINGS OF ITS FEATURES FROM BEHIND THE UNREASONING MASK--IN MOBY DICK IS OUTRAGEOUS STRENGTH, WITH AN INSCRUTABLE MALICE SINEWING IT!"

"I'LL CHASE HIM ROUND GOOD HOPE," HE FURIED, "AND ROUND THE NORWAY MAELSTROM, AND ROUND PERDITION'S FLAMES BEFORE I GIVE HIM UP. AND THIS IS WHAT YE HAVE SHIPPED FOR, TO CHASE THAT WHITE WHALE ON BOTH SIDES OF LAND AND OVER ALL SIDES OF THE EARTH, TILL HE SPOUTS BLACK BLOOD AND ROLLS FIN OUT."

ONLY STARBUCK DID NOT DRINK TO OUR TOAST THAT DAY. "GOD HURT US ALL, IF WE DO NOT HUNT MOBY DICK TO HIS DEATH..."

WINNING US CREW TO HIS VIEWS WAS EASIER THAN AHAB HAD FEARED IT WOULD BE.

"WHAT I'VE DARED, I'VE WILLED; AND WHAT I'VE WILLED I'LL DO!" HE MARVELED.

"THEY THINK ME MAD-- STARBUCK DOES; BUT I'M DEMONIAC, I AM MADNESS MADDENED! THAT WILD MADNESS THAT'S ONLY CALM TO COMPREHEND ITSELF!"

EACH NIGHT THEN AHAB WOULD SPEND LONG HOURS ON HIS CHARTS, WORKING OUT THE ROUTES OF THE GREAT SPERM WHALES-- WHAT WAS CALLED THEIR "VEINS".

HE WOULD WORK UNDER A SWINGING LAMP, THE LIGHT CASTING HIGHLIGHTS AND SHADOWS ON AHAB'S BROW TILL IT ALMOST SEEMED THAT WHILE HE WAS MAKING OUTLINES AND COURSES ON THE WRINKLED CHARTS...

...SOME INVISIBLE PENCIL WAS ALSO TRACING LINES AND COURSES UPON THE DEEPLY MARKED CHART OF HIS FOREHEAD.

WHILE AHAB SKULKED IN HIS CABIN, TALES OF HIS WHITE WHALE RAN RAMPANT ACROSS THE DECK...

OF HIS PECULIAR SNOW WHITE FOREHEAD AND A HIGH, PYRAMIDICAL WHITE HUMP...

OF THAT UNEXAMPLED, INTELLIGENT *MALIGNITY*...

THAT TO MANY PEOPLE HE HAD SEVERAL TIMES BEEN KNOWN TO TURN ROUND SUDDENLY, AND BEARING DOWN UPON THEM, EITHER STAVE THEIR BOATS TO SPLINTERS, OR DRIVE THEM BACK IN CONSTERNATION TO THEIR SHIP...

AND THAT AHAB SAW MOBY DICK AS THE MONOMANIAC INCARNATION OF ALL THOSE MALICIOUS AGENCIES FOUND IN THE UNIVERSE-- EVIL FORCES AHAB MUST DESTROY IN ORDER TO SURVIVE AS A FREE MAN.

AND WHILE WE TALKED ABOVE, PHANTOM, SHADOWY VOICES OF SOMEBODIES NOT YET SEEN ON DECK HISSED BELOW...

·12·

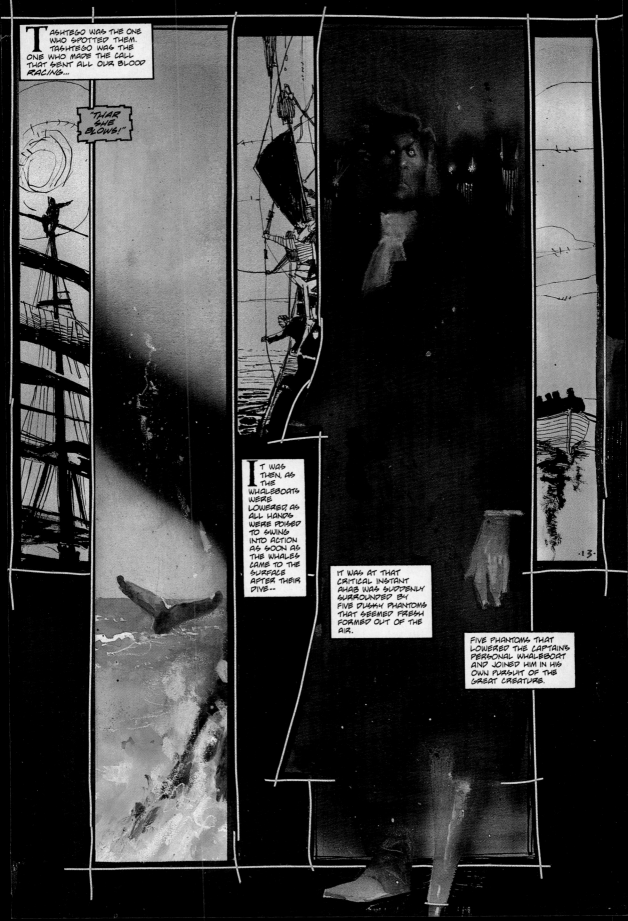

TASHTEGO WAS THE ONE WHO SPOTTED THEM. TASHTEGO WAS THE ONE WHO MADE THE CALL THAT SENT ALL OUR BLOOD *RACING*...

"THAR SHE BLOWS!"

IT WAS THEN, AS THE WHALEBOATS WERE LOWERED, AS ALL HANDS WERE POISED TO SWING INTO ACTION AS SOON AS THE WHALES CAME TO THE SURFACE AFTER THEIR DIVE--

IT WAS AT THAT CRITICAL INSTANT AHAB WAS SUDDENLY SURROUNDED BY FIVE DUSKY PHANTOMS THAT SEEMED FRESH FORMED OUT OF THE AIR.

FIVE PHANTOMS THAT LOWERED THE CAPTAIN'S PERSONAL WHALEBOAT AND JOINED HIM IN HIS OWN PURSUIT OF THE GREAT CREATURE.

-13-

THE FOUR BOATS RACED FURIOUSLY FOR THE WHALES--

STARBUCK WHISPERING DIRECT, EARNEST EXHORTATIONS TO HIS MEN...

STUBB'S COMMANDS COMPOUNDED OF FUN AND FURY...

NO HARPOONER STRUCK THE WHALES, HOWEVER, AND A STORM BROKE, SHROUDING US IN FOG--

FLASK ROARING HIS MEN BEACH THEIR BOAT ON A WHALE'S BACK...

-- OUT OF WHICH THE PEQUOD SUDDENLY APPEARED, BEARING DOWN ON US TO GRIND OUR WHALEBOAT TO PIECES AS WE LEAPT TO SAFETY!

THERE IS NOTHING LIKE THE PERILS OF WHALING TO BREED A FREE AND EASY SORT OF GENIAL, DESPERADO PHILOSOPHY.

WE SOON LEARNED THE IDENTITY OF AHAB'S PHANTOMS.

LED BY AN AGING ORIENTAL NAMED FEDALLAH, THEY WERE PARSEE-- A RACE NOTORIOUS FOR A CERTAIN DIABOLISM OF SUBTILTY, AND SUPPOSED BY SOME HONEST WHITE MARINERS TO BE THE PAID SPIES AND SECRET CONFIDENTIAL AGENTS ON THE WATER OF THE DEVIL...

FEDALLAH WAS A WORSHIPPER OF ZOROASTER, WHICH TOLD ITS FOLLOWERS THAT MAN WAS DESTINED TO CHOOSE BETWEEN GOOD AND EVIL, LIGHT AND DARKNESS.

SOME SAID FEDALLAH WAS THE DEVIL, GOADING AHAB'S ALREADY TORMENTED SOUL TO PLUNGE EVER-FORWARD IN HIS PERSONAL STRUGGLE WITH EVIL.

PERHAPS. PERHAPS NOT. FEDALLAH WAS, AND WOULD REMAIN, A MUFFLED MYSTERY TO THE LAST.

SOUTHEAST OF THE CAPE, WE PASSED ANOTHER NANTUCKET WHALER, THE ALBATROSS. THERE WAS SOME HOPE OF A GAM--A MEETING OF TWO SHIPS WHERE NEWS IS EXCHANGED AND A SOCIAL VISIT MADE.

AS OUR TWO SHIPS CAME ABREAST, AHAB CALLED, "SHIP AHOY! HAVE YE SEEN THE WHITE WHALE?!" BUT WHEN THE CAPTAIN OF THE ALBATROSS RAISED HIS TRUMPET TO ANSWER, IT SUDDENLY FELL FROM HIS HANDS, VANISHING INTO THE SEA.

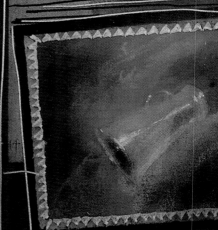

IT WAS AHAB'S CUSTOM NOT TO JOIN IN A GAM WITH ANY SHIP THAT DID NOT BOAST KNOWLEDGE OF MOBY DICK, BUT WITH THE WHALER TOWN-HO THE CAPTAIN RELENTED AND THERE WAS A REGULAR GAM.

WE SAILED ON, SPYING WHAT WE BELIEVED TO BE MOBY DICK AND INSTEAD FINDING IT TO BE A GIANT SQUID--A SIGHT FEW WHALE SHIPS EVER BEHELD AND RETURNED TO THEIR PORTS TO TELL OF...

BUT QUEEQUEG SAID THAT WHERE THERE WAS SQUID THERE WAS SPERM WHALE--AND THERE WAS, OF A SUDDEN, SWIMMING LAZILY NOT 100 YARDS AWAY!

...AND IT WAS OURS.

EVER TOLD TO APTAIN AHAB AS THE SECRET ALE OF THE OWN-HO--HOW HE WHITE WHALE HAD PPEARED LIKE OME SORT OF IVINE JUSTICE STEAD OF HIS XPECTED DARK VIL, RIGHTING WRONG BY EVOURING A UTINOUS HALER.

THE 1200-FOOT-LONG WHALE LINES WERE TIED TO THE HARPOONS, TWO IN EACH WHALEBOAT LYING IN A NOTCHED STICK CALLED A CROTCH. TWO, TO BE THROWN IN QUICK SUCCESSION--IN CASE ONE SHOULD PULL FROM THE WHALE, THE OTHER WOULD BE SECURE.

THE HARPOONERS PULLED OAR TOWARD THE WHALE, PREPARING TO THROW THE DART--THE PIERCING OF THE WHALE WITH THE HARPOON. WHEN THE MOMENT ARRIVED, THE HARPOONER DROPPED OAR, SECURED IT, TURNED AROUND AND FLUNG HIS METAL AT THE CREATURE...

STUBB WAS OVERJOYED, BUT AHAB RETIRED MOODILY TO HIS CABIN. A WHALE WAS KILLED-- A GREAT SPERM WHALE.

BUT MOBY DICK STILL LIVED.

THE CRY WENT UP--
"SAIL HO!"--AND WE
SOON FOUND
OURSELVES ALONGSIDE THE
JEROBOAM OF NANTUCKET.

BUT THERE WAS TO
BE NO SOCIAL GAM--
AN EPIDEMIC THAT
HELD THE JEROBOAM
KEPT OUR MEETING
TO JUST-HEARD
SHOUTS ACROSS
ROUGH SEAS...

...AND OVER THE MAD SHRIEKS OF A CRAZED
ZEALOT ABOARD THE JEROBOAM, THINKING
HIMSELF THE ARCHANGEL GABRIEL AND
PROCLAIMING MOBY DICK TO BE A SHAKER
GOD REINCARNATED.

BETWEEN GABRIEL'S WILD CRIES, THE
JEROBOAM'S CAPTAIN, MAYHEW, TOLD
AHAB THEY HAD INDEED SEEN THE
WHITE WHALE--WITH HIS MASSIVE TAIL,
MOBY DICK HAD CRUSHED THE
JEROBOAM'S MATE, HARRY MACEY.

AHAB REMEMBERED HE
HAD A LETTER FOR THE
DEAD MACEY, AND SENT
IT DOWN TO MAYHEW ON
THE END OF A CUTTING
SPADE.

BUT GABRIEL SEIZED
THE LETTER, IMPALED
IT ON A KNIFE AND
THREW IT ONTO THE
PEQUOD'S DECK,
GABRIEL SCREECHING...

"NAY, KEEP
IT THYSELF...
THOU ART
SOON GOING
MACEY'S WAY!"

WITH THE HEAD OF A SPERM WHALE AFFIXED TO ONE SIDE OF THE PEQUOD, AHAB THEN COMMANDED THAT A RIGHT WHALE BE CAPTURED.

THIS CAME AS A SURPRISE TO ALL, SINCE THE RIGHT WHALE'S OIL WAS FOUL... OR, AS STUBB PUT IT, THE RIGHT WAS A "LUMP OF FOUL LARD."

AFTER THE WHALE WAS KILLED, I LOOKED DOWN AT THOSE TWO HEADS STRAPPED TO THE SHIP, TWO SO DIFFERENT, BALANCED AGAINST EACH OTHER-- THE RIGHT WHALE'S LIKE AN OLD DUTCH SHOE, THE SPERM'S FOREHEAD PERVADING DIGNITY AND BATTERING-RAM POWER.

FLASK, MEANWHILE, EXPLAINED TO STUBB THAT FEDALLAH HAD CONVINCED AHAB A SHIP WITH A SPERM WHALE'S HEAD ON THE STARBOARD SIDE AND A RIGHT WHALE'S HEAD ON THE PORT COULD NEVER CAPSIZE.

STUBB ASSERTED THAT FEDALLAH WAS THE DEVIL, AND THAT HE, STUBB, WOULD HEAVE HIM OVERBOARD IF HE GOT THE OPPORTUNITY.

AS FOR MYSELF, I HAD BEGUN TO NOTICE THAT THE PARSEE HAD DEVELOPED THE HABIT OF STANDING IN AHAB'S SHADOW, SO AS TO CAST NONE OF HIS OWN.

THE DEVIL, OF COURSE, IS SAID TO HAVE *NO SHADOW...*

17

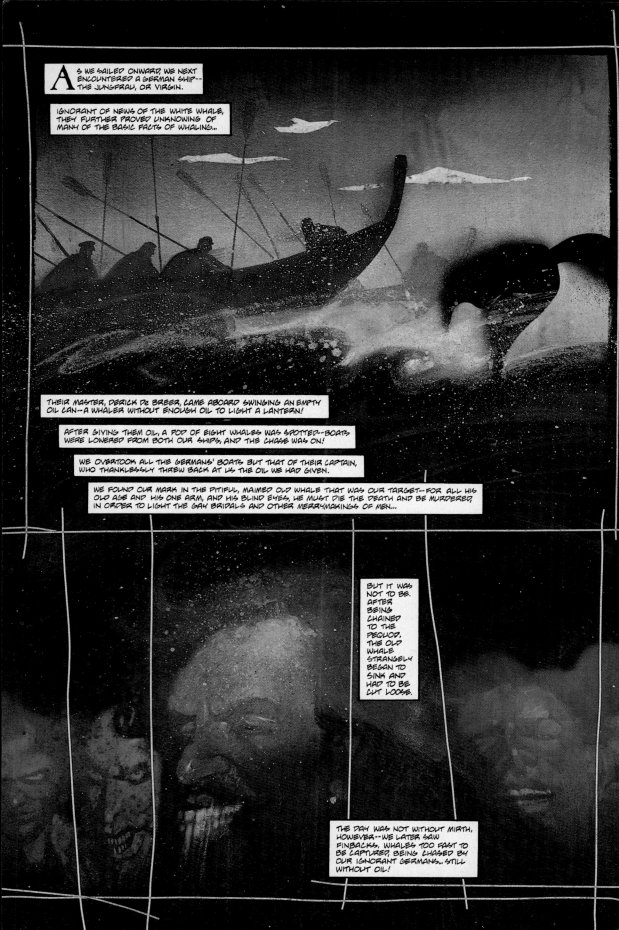

AS WE SAILED ONWARD, WE NEXT ENCOUNTERED A GERMAN SHIP-- THE JUNGFRAU, OR VIRGIN.

IGNORANT OF NEWS OF THE WHITE WHALE, THEY FURTHER PROVED UNKNOWING OF MANY OF THE BASIC FACTS OF WHALING...

THEIR MASTER, DERICK De BREER, CAME ABOARD SWINGING AN EMPTY OIL CAN--A WHALER WITHOUT ENOUGH OIL TO LIGHT A LANTERN!

AFTER GIVING THEM OIL, A POD OF EIGHT WHALES WAS SPOTTED--BOATS WERE LOWERED FROM BOTH OUR SHIPS, AND THE CHASE WAS ON!

WE OVERTOOK ALL THE GERMANS' BOATS BUT THAT OF THEIR CAPTAIN, WHO THANKLESSLY THREW BACK AT US THE OIL WE HAD GIVEN.

WE FOUND OUR MARK IN THE PITIFUL, MAIMED OLD WHALE THAT WAS OUR TARGET--FOR ALL HIS OLD AGE AND HIS ONE ARM, AND HIS BLIND EYES, HE MUST DIE THE DEATH AND BE MURDERED, IN ORDER TO LIGHT THE GAY BRIDALS AND OTHER MERRY-MAKINGS OF MEN...

BUT IT WAS NOT TO BE. AFTER BEING CHAINED TO THE PEQUOD, THE OLD WHALE STRANGELY BEGAN TO SINK AND HAD TO BE CUT LOOSE.

THE DAY WAS NOT WITHOUT MIRTH, HOWEVER--WE LATER SAW FINBACKS, WHALES TOO FAST TO BE CAPTURED, BEING CHASED BY OUR IGNORANT GERMANS... STILL WITHOUT OIL!

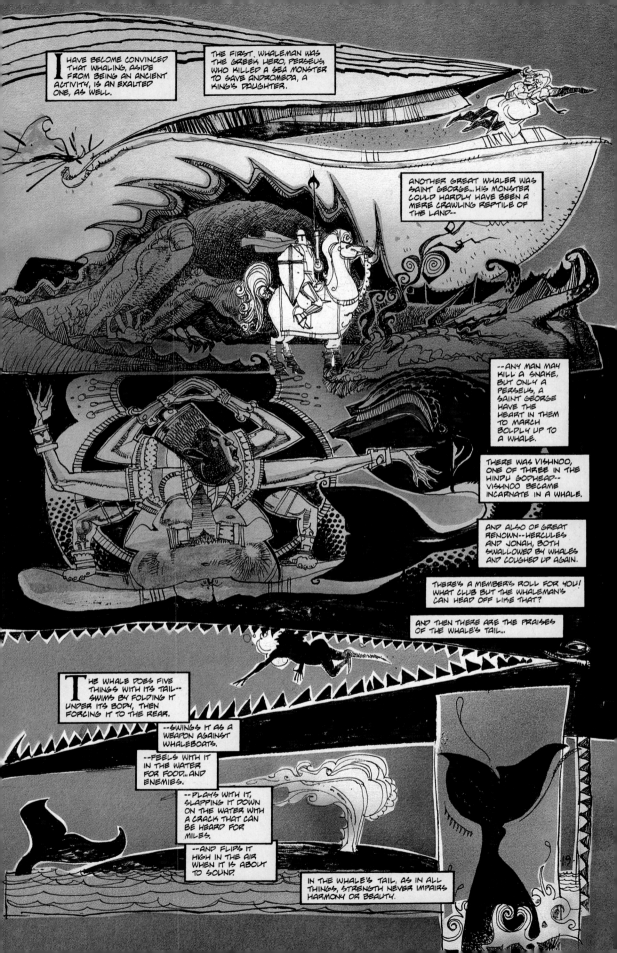

I HAVE BECOME CONVINCED THAT WHALING, ASIDE FROM BEING AN ANCIENT ACTIVITY, IS AN EXALTED ONE, AS WELL.

THE FIRST WHALEMAN WAS THE GREEK HERO, PERSEUS, WHO KILLED A SEA MONSTER TO SAVE ANDROMEDA, A KING'S DAUGHTER.

ANOTHER GREAT WHALER WAS SAINT GEORGE... HIS MONSTER COULD HARDLY HAVE BEEN A MERE CRAWLING REPTILE OF THE LAND--

--ANY MAN MAY KILL A SNAKE, BUT ONLY A PERSEUS, A SAINT GEORGE HAVE THE HEART IN THEM TO MARCH BOLDLY UP TO A WHALE.

THERE WAS VISHNOO, ONE OF THREE IN THE HINDU GODHEAD-- VISHNOO BECAME INCARNATE IN A WHALE.

AND ALSO OF GREAT RENOWN--HERCULES AND JONAH, BOTH SWALLOWED BY WHALES AND COUGHED UP AGAIN.

THERE'S A MEMBER'S ROLL FOR YOU! WHAT CLUB BUT THE WHALEMAN'S CAN HEAD OFF LIKE THAT?

AND THEN THERE ARE THE PRAISES OF THE WHALE'S TAIL...

THE WHALE DOES FIVE THINGS WITH ITS TAIL-- SWIMS BY FOLDING IT UNDER ITS BODY, THEN FORCING IT TO THE REAR.

--SWINGS IT AS A WEAPON AGAINST WHALEBOATS.

--FEELS WITH IT IN THE WATER FOR FOOD... AND ENEMIES.

--PLAYS WITH IT, SLAPPING IT DOWN ON THE WATER WITH A CRACK THAT CAN BE HEARD FOR MILES.

--AND FLIPS IT HIGH IN THE AIR WHEN IT IS ABOUT TO SOUND.

IN THE WHALE'S TAIL, AS IN ALL THINGS, STRENGTH NEVER IMPAIRS HARMONY OR BEAUTY.

WE LEFT THE INDIAN OCEAN, JOURNEYED THROUGH THE STRAITS OF SUNDA, BOUND FOR THE CHINA SEA.

IN THE STRAITS, WE CAME UPON AN ENORMOUS SCHOOL OF WHALES--NORMALLY TWENTY OR FIFTY IN NUMBER, THIS ONE RANGED IN THE HUNDREDS, A GRAND ARMADA.

THERE WERE TWO TYPES OF SCHOOLS...THE FEMALES, ATTENDED BY ONE FULL-GROWN MALE, BOTH HUSBAND AND GUARDIAN TO HIS HAREM BEFORE GROWING OLD AND TAKING THE SOLITARY LIFE--

--AND THE YOUNG BULLS, LIKE A MOB OF YOUNG COLLEGIANS, ROLLICKING AND RESTLESS... THEY ARE MORE DANGEROUS TO ENCOUNTER THAN MOST WHALES.

THE MOST DANGEROUS OF ALL WERE THOSE WONDROUS GREY-HEADED, GRIZZLED WHALES, SOMETIMES MET, AND THESE WILL FIGHT YOU LIKE GRIM FRIENDS--MOBY DICK WAS SUCH A WHALE.

WE HAD SETTLED INTO AN UNEVENTFUL ROUTINE, WHEN WE WERE GREETED BY THE FOUL STENCH OF A DEAD AND ROTTING WHALE.

THE BOUTON-de-ROSE, A FRENCH SHIP, HAD FASTENED TWO BLASTED WHALES TO ITS SIDES--WHALES THAT HAD DIED UNCAPTURED AT SEA.

NICKNAMING THE FRENCH SHIP "THE ROSEBUD," STUBB CONSPIRED WITH THE SHIP'S ENGLISH-SPEAKING MATE TO SPARE THE ROSEBUD'S CREW THE DIRTY SCRAPE OF CUTTING UP THE STINKING WHALES...TRANSLATING STUBB'S INSULTS INTO DIRE WARNINGS OF DISEASE, THE MATE CONVINCED THE FRENCH CAPTAIN TO CUT THE WHALES LOOSE.

STUBB GRACIOUSLY OFFERED TO TOW THE CARCASSES AWAY--AND THEN GREEDILY DUG HIS HANDS INTO THEM, COMING UP WITH HANDFULS OF PRECIOUS AMBERGRIS.

USED IN THE FINEST PERFUMES AND TO FLAVOR THE CLARET OF CERTAIN WINES, IT FORMED IN THE BOWELS ONLY OF THE SICK AND DYING WHALE.

A RARE AND FRAGRANT TREASURE FOUND ONLY WHEN THE WHALE SMELLS HIS WORST.

20

SOON AFTER, ONE OF STUBB'S OARSMEN HURT HIS HAND, SO THE LITTLE NEGRO BOY, PIP--A GAY, HAPPY FELLOW WHO LOVED LIFE AND ALL LIFE'S PEACEABLE SECURITIES--WENT INTO THE BOAT IN HIS PLACE.

LEAPING AT A JOLT FROM A WHALE, PIP BECAME TANGLED IN THE WHALE LINE--STUBB ORDERED THE LINE CUT AND THE WHALE ESCAPED.

STRUCK WITH PITY FOR THE CHILD, AHAB TURNED HIS FACE HEAVENWARDS, CRYING IN DEFIANCE, "OH, YE FROZEN HEAVENS! LOOK DOWN HERE. YE DID BEGET THIS LUCKLESS CHILD AND HAVE ABANDONED HIM, YE CREATIVE LIBERTINES."

AHAB CONTINUED, "SEE THE OMNISCIENT GODS OBLIVIOUS OF SUFFERING MAN; AND MAN, THOUGH IDIOTIC, AND KNOWING NOT WHAT HE DOES, YET, FULL OF THE SWEET THINGS OF LOVE AND GRATITUDE."

DECLARING THAT PIP WOULD NOW NEVER LEAVE HIS SIDE AND WOULD LIVE WITH HIM IN HIS CABIN, AHAB WHISPERED SOFTLY, "THOU TOUCHEST MY INMOST CENTRE BOY; THOU ART TIED TO ME BY CORDS WOVEN OF MY HEART-STRINGS."

"STAY IN THE BOAT!" DEMANDED STUBB IN A RAGE, PROMISING PIP THAT IF HE JUMPED AGAIN, HE WOULD BE LEFT BEHIND.

AND PIP *DID* JUMP AGAIN...

LEFT ALONE FOR HOURS BEFORE THE PEQUOD RESCUED HIM BY CHANCE...

LEFT ALONE IN THE OCEAN WHERE THE AWFUL LONESOMENESS IS INTOLERABLE...THE INTENSE CONCENTRATION OF SELF IN THE MIDDLE OF SUCH A HEARTLESS IMMENSITY WAS TOO MUCH FOR THE YOUNG NEGRO BOY, AND HE LOST HIS MIND.

AS THEY WENT, A CREWMAN WAS HEARD TO SAY, "THERE GO TWO DAFT ONES NOW. ONE DAFT WITH *STRENGTH*, THE OTHER WITH *WEAKNESS*."

21

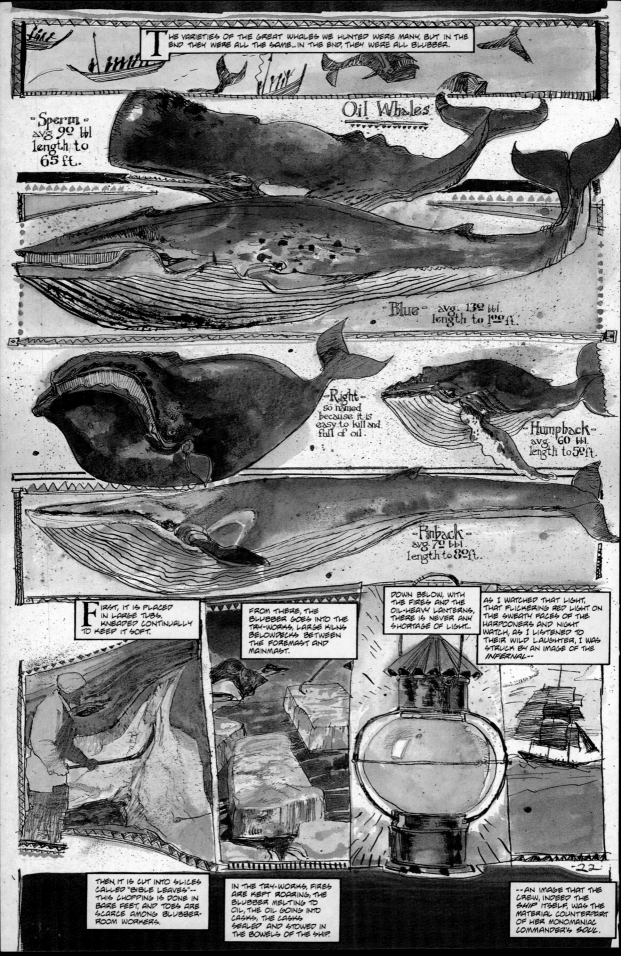

THE VARIETIES OF THE GREAT WHALES WE HUNTED WERE MANY, BUT IN THE END THEY WERE ALL THE SAME...IN THE END, THEY WERE ALL BLUBBER.

Oil Whales

- Sperm -
avg 90 bbl
length to
65 ft.

- Blue - avg. 130 bbl.
length to 100 ft.

- Right -
so named
because it is
easy to kill and
full of oil.

- Humpback -
avg. 60 bbl.
length to 50 ft.

- Finback -
avg. 70 bbl.
length to 80 ft.

FIRST, IT IS PLACED IN LARGE TUBS, KNEADED CONTINUALLY TO KEEP IT SOFT.

FROM THERE, THE BLUBBER GOES INTO THE TRY-WORKS, LARGE KILNS BELOWDECKS BETWEEN THE FOREMAST AND MAINMAST.

DOWN BELOW, WITH THE FIRES AND THE OIL-HEAVY LANTERNS, THERE IS NEVER ANY SHORTAGE OF LIGHT...

AS I WATCHED THAT LIGHT, THAT FLICKERING RED LIGHT ON THE SWEATY FACES OF THE HARPOONERS AND NIGHT WATCH, AS I LISTENED TO THEIR WILD LAUGHTER, I WAS STRUCK BY AN IMAGE OF THE INFERNAL--

THEN, IT IS CUT INTO SLICES CALLED "BIBLE LEAVES"-- THIS CHOPPING IS DONE IN BARE FEET, AND TOES ARE SCARCE AMONG BLUBBER-ROOM WORKERS.

IN THE TRY-WORKS, FIRES ARE KEPT ROARING, THE BLUBBER MELTING TO OIL, THE OIL GOING INTO CASKS, THE CASKS SEALED AND STOWED IN THE BOWELS OF THE SHIP.

--AN IMAGE THAT THE CREW, INDEED THE SHIP ITSELF, WAS THE MATERIAL COUNTERPART OF HER MONOMANIAC COMMANDER'S SOUL.

AHAB'S GOLD DOUBLOON, HIS REWARD FOR THE WHALER MAKING THE FIRST SIGHTING OF MOBY DICK, CONTINUED TO SHINE OUT FROM THE MAST, AN UNEASY REMINDER OF WHERE OUR JOURNEY IS TAKING US...

A JOURNEY COMING THAT MUCH CLOSER TO ITS END AS WE MET AN ENGLISH SHIP, THE SAMUEL ENDERBY...

"SHIP AHOY! HAST THOU SEEN THE WHITE WHALE?" AHAB CRIED OUT.

"SEE HOW *THIS?*"

SEEING NEW EVIDENCE OF HIS QUARRY'S MALICE, AHAB QUICKLY RUSHED TO BOARD THE ENDERBY, A LARGE HOOK RAISING AHAB UP TO WHERE HIS ONE GOOD LEG COULD NOT TAKE HIM.

THERE, AHAB AND BOOMER, THE ENDERBY'S CAPTAIN, SHARED A SPECIAL HANDSHAKE--BOTH MEMBERS IN A SELECT, THOUGH UNENVIABLE, CLUB.

CAPTAIN BOOMER TOLD OF SPOTTING THE WHITE WHALE AT THE LINE-- THE EQUATOR--BUT WARNED THAT MOBY DICK WAS "BEST LET ALONE."

"WHAT IS BEST LET ALONE, THAT ACCURSED THING IS NOT ALWAYS WHAT LEAST ALLURES", AHAB COUNTERED.

"HE'S ALL MAGNET," HE EXCLAIMED, MEANING MOBY DICK... AND AHAB WAS DETERMINED THAT HE WOULD BE DRAWN TO THE BEAST.

23

IN HIS HASTE TO LEAVE THE ENDERBY, AHAB CRACKED HIS IVORY LIMB, AND ORDERED THE SHIP'S CARPENTER TO FASHION HIM A NEW ONE.

THE CARPENTER SNEEZED AS THE DUST FROM THE DRY BONE HE FILED FOR AHAB'S LEG CHOKED HIM... HE WAS A PURE MANIPULATOR; HIS BRAIN, IF HE EVER HAD ONE, MUST HAVE EARLY OOZED ALONG INTO THE MUSCLES OF HIS FINGERS--HE WAS REMARKABLE ONLY FOR A CERTAIN IMPERSONAL STOLIDITY.

AHAB, FOR HIS PART IN THE ENTERPRISE, IRONICALLY ADDRESSED THE CARPENTER AS "MANMAKER," AND CURSED HIS OWN DEPENDENCE ON ANYONE ELSE FOR ANY SERVICE.

"HERE I AM, PROUD AS A GREEK GOD, AND YET STANDING DEBTOR TO THIS BLOCKHEAD FOR A BONE TO STAND ON! CURSED BE THAT MORAL INTER-INDEBTEDNESS WHICH WILL NOT DO AWAY WITH LEDGERS.

"I WOULD BE FREE AS AIR; AND I'M DOWN IN THE WORLD'S BOOKS. I AM SO RICH, I COULD HAVE GIVEN BID FOR BID WITH THE WEALTHIEST PRAETORIANS AT THE AUCTION OF THE ROMAN EMPIRE... AND YET I OWE FOR THE FLESH IN THE TONGUE I BRAG WITH."

TWICE A WEEK, THE HOLD IN WHICH THE OIL CASKS WERE KEPT WAS FLOODED WITH SEA WATER TO CHECK FOR LEAKS.

FINDING EVIDENCE OF OIL ESCAPING STARBUCK WENT TO AHAB'S CABIN TO URGE THAT THE CASKS BE REMOVED FROM THE HOLD TO DETERMINE THE SOURCE OF THE LEAK.

LOST IN HIS CHARTS AND WANTING NOTHING TO DELAY THE HUNT, AHAB WHIRLED ON HIS MATE, REFUSING. WHEN STARBUCK INSISTED, AHAB GRABBED A MUSKET, THUNDERING--

"THERE IS ONE GOD THAT IS LORD OVER THE EARTH, AND ONE CAPTAIN THAT IS LORD OVER THE PEQUOD-- ON DECK WITH YOU!"

STARBUCK TOOK HIS LEAVE THEN, BUT NOT BEFORE CRYING OUT--

"THOU HAS OUTRAGED, NOT INSULTED ME, SIR. BUT FOR THAT I ASK THEE NOT TO BEWARE OF STARBUCK-- THOU WOULDST BUT LAUGH-- BUT LET AHAB BEWARE OF AHAB; BEWARE OF THYSELF, OLD MAN."

AHAB LONG CONSIDERED STARBUCK'S WORDS... AND THEN ORDERED THE HOLD OPENED AND THE CASKS EXAMINED.

25

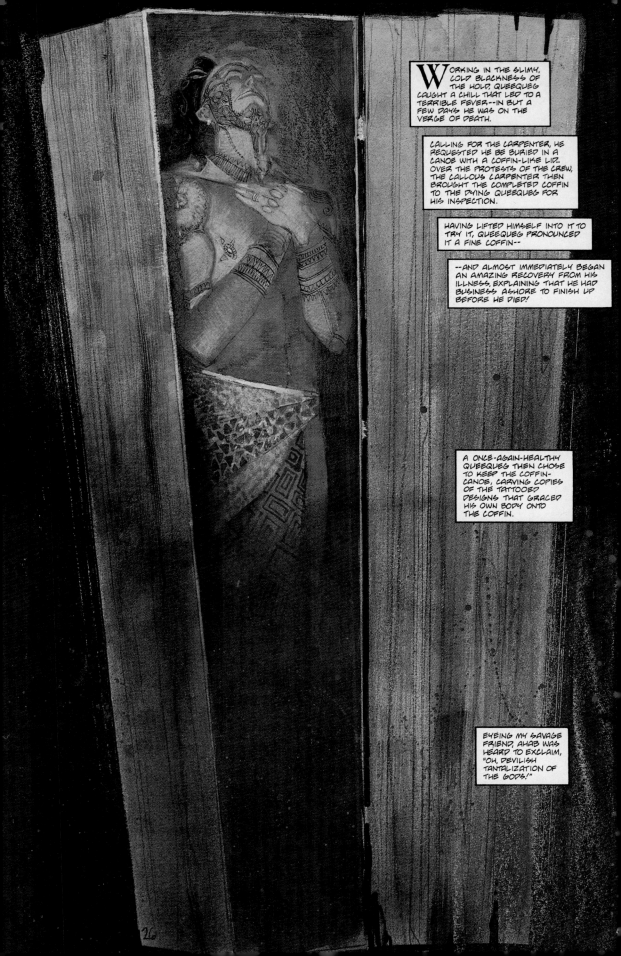

WORKING IN THE SLIMY, COLD BLACKNESS OF THE HOLD, QUEEQUEG CAUGHT A CHILL THAT LED TO A TERRIBLE FEVER--IN BUT A FEW DAYS HE WAS ON THE VERGE OF DEATH.

CALLING FOR THE CARPENTER, HE REQUESTED HE BE BURIED IN A CANOE WITH A COFFIN-LIKE LID. OVER THE PROTESTS OF THE CREW, THE CALLOUS CARPENTER THEN BROUGHT THE COMPLETED COFFIN TO THE DYING QUEEQUEG FOR HIS INSPECTION.

HAVING LIFTED HIMSELF INTO IT TO TRY IT, QUEEQUEG PRONOUNCED IT A FINE COFFIN--

--AND ALMOST IMMEDIATELY BEGAN AN AMAZING RECOVERY FROM HIS ILLNESS, EXPLAINING THAT HE HAD BUSINESS ASHORE TO FINISH UP BEFORE HE DIED!

A ONCE-AGAIN-HEALTHY QUEEQUEG THEN CHOSE TO KEEP THE COFFIN-CANOE, CARVING COPIES OF THE TATTOOED DESIGNS THAT GRACED HIS OWN BODY ONTO THE COFFIN.

EYEING MY SAVAGE FRIEND, AHAB WAS HEARD TO EXCLAIM, "OH, DEVILISH TANTALIZATION OF THE GODS!"

26

THE PEQUOD'S BLACKSMITH'S NAME WAS PERTH, A ONCE-WELL-TO-DO ENGLISHMAN, HIS FAMILY AND FORTUNE LOST TO DRINK.

SILENT, SLOW AND SOLEMN; BOWING OVER STILL FURTHER HIS CHRONICALLY BROKEN BACK, HE TOILED AWAY AS IF TOIL WERE LIFE ITSELF, AND THE HEAVY BEATING OF HIS HAMMER, THE HEAVY BEATING OF HIS HEART. AND SO IT WAS--MOST MISERABLE!

AHAB APPROACHED THE SMITH'S FORGE WITH NAILS OF HARDEST IRON, ASKING PERTH TO HELP HIM FORGE A HARPOON POINT WHICH WOULD PIERCE THE FLESH OF ANY WHALE.

WITH THE FORGE RUNNING HOT ABOUT THEM, AHAB ASKED PERTH WHY HE WAS NOT BURNED BY THE FLYING SPARKS. "I AM PAST SCORCHING;" THE SMITH REPLIED. "NOT EASILY CAN'ST THOU SCORCH A SCAR."

AHAB THEN ASKED PERTH IF HE COULD SMOOTH THE SEAMS OF MISERY IN AHAB'S BROWS, FOR AHAB WOULD GLADLY LAY HIS HEAD TO ANVIL TO HAVE IT DONE.

"OH! THAT IS THE ONE, SIR!" PERTH EXCLAIMED. "SAID I NOT ALL SEAMS AND DENTS BUT ONE?"

FORGING RAZOR BLADES IN PLACE AS BARBS, THE HARPOON STOOD ALMOST COMPLETE...ALL THAT REMAINED WAS TO TEMPER THE RED-HOT POINT.

--TEMPER IT IN BLOOD DONATED BY THE THREE HARPOONERS.

THE RED-HOT POINT PLUNGED INTO THE WARM RED AS AHAB SPOKE THE WORDS, "EGO NON BAPTIZO TE IN NOMINE PATRIS, SED IN NOMINE DIABOLI!"

BAPTIZING THE HARPOON IN THE NAME OF THE *DEVIL*...

27

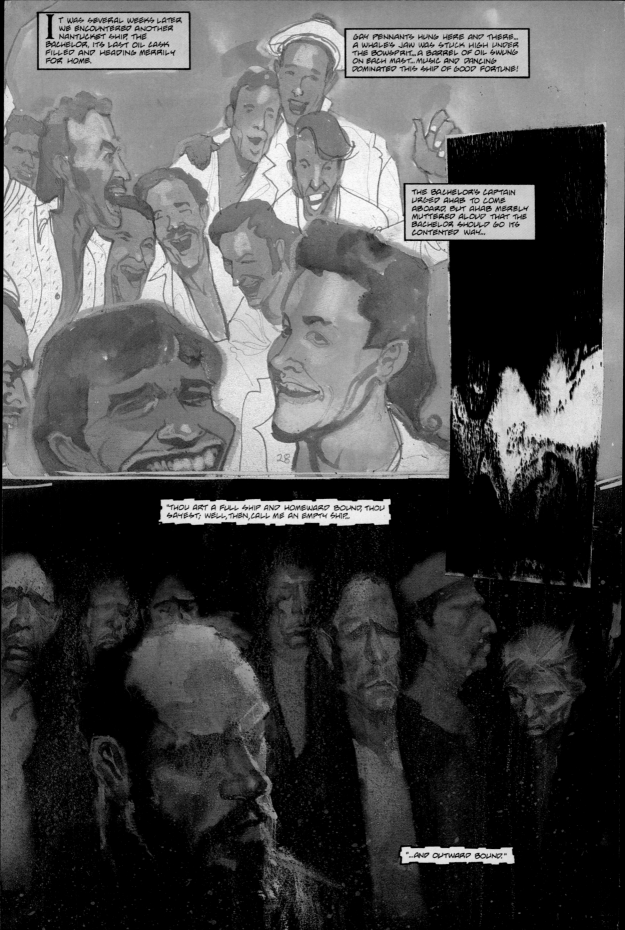

IT WAS SEVERAL WEEKS LATER WE ENCOUNTERED ANOTHER NANTUCKET SHIP, THE BACHELOR, ITS LAST OIL CASK FILLED AND HEADING MERRILY FOR HOME.

GAY PENNANTS HUNG HERE AND THERE... A WHALE'S JAW WAS STUCK HIGH UNDER THE BOWSPRIT... A BARREL OF OIL SWUNG ON EACH MAST... MUSIC AND DANCING DOMINATED THIS SHIP OF GOOD FORTUNE!

THE BACHELOR'S CAPTAIN URGED AHAB TO COME ABOARD, BUT AHAB MERELY MUTTERED ALOUD THAT THE BACHELOR SHOULD GO ITS CONTENTED WAY...

"THOU ART A FULL SHIP AND HOMEWARD BOUND, THOU SAYEST; WELL, THEN, CALL ME AN EMPTY SHIP...

"...AND OUTWARD BOUND."

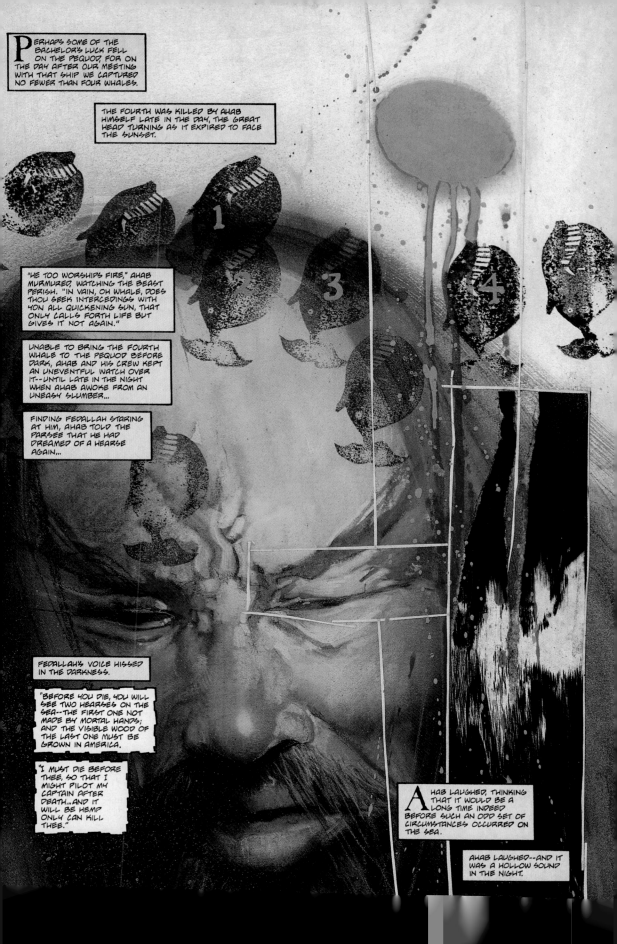

PERHAPS SOME OF THE BACHELOR'S LUCK FELL ON THE PEQUOD, FOR ON THE DAY AFTER OUR MEETING WITH THAT SHIP WE CAPTURED NO FEWER THAN FOUR WHALES.

THE FOURTH WAS KILLED BY AHAB HIMSELF LATE IN THE DAY, THE GREAT HEAD TURNING AS IT EXPIRED TO FACE THE SUNSET.

"HE TOO WORSHIPS FIRE," AHAB MURMURED, WATCHING THE BEAST PERISH. "IN VAIN, OH WHALE, DOES THOU SEEK INTERCEDINGS WITH YON ALL QUICKENING SUN, THAT ONLY CALLS FORTH LIFE BUT GIVES IT NOT AGAIN."

UNABLE TO BRING THE FOURTH WHALE TO THE PEQUOD BEFORE DARK, AHAB AND HIS CREW KEPT AN UNEVENTFUL WATCH OVER IT--UNTIL LATE IN THE NIGHT WHEN AHAB AWOKE FROM AN UNEASY SLUMBER...

FINDING FEDALLAH STARING AT HIM, AHAB TOLD THE PARSEE THAT HE HAD DREAMED OF A HEARSE AGAIN...

FEDALLAH'S VOICE HISSED IN THE DARKNESS.

"BEFORE YOU DIE, YOU WILL SEE TWO HEARSES ON THE SEA--THE FIRST ONE NOT MADE BY MORTAL HANDS; AND THE VISIBLE WOOD OF THE LAST ONE MUST BE GROWN IN AMERICA.

"I MUST DIE BEFORE THEE, SO THAT I MIGHT PILOT MY CAPTAIN AFTER DEATH...AND IT WILL BE HEMP ONLY CAN KILL THEE."

AHAB LAUGHED, THINKING THAT IT WOULD BE A LONG TIME INDEED BEFORE SUCH AN ODD SET OF CIRCUMSTANCES OCCURRED ON THE SEA.

AHAB LAUGHED--AND IT WAS A HOLLOW SOUND IN THE NIGHT.

AHAB STEERED THE SHIP FOR THE LINE IN SEARCH OF HIS GREAT WHALE, USING THE QUADRANT TO TAKE THE SHIP'S POSITION FROM THE SUN.

BUT THE SUN COULD ONLY TELL AHAB WHERE HE WAS--NOT WHERE HE WOULD BE OR, MOST IMPORTANTLY, WHERE THE WHITE WHALE WAS.

"CURSE THEE, THY VAIN TOY!" HE SHOUTED, SMASHING THE QUADRANT. "CURSED BE ALL THINGS THAT CAST MAN'S EYES ALOFT TO THAT HEAVEN, WHOSE LIVE VIVIDNESS BUT SCORCHES HIM!"

FROM THEN ON WE WOULD STEER ONLY BY THE COMPASS AND OUR SPEED--BY DEAD RECKONING.

IN THE PACIFIC, THE WORST OF ALL SEA STORMS-- THE TYPHOON--CAN COME UPON A SHIP WITHIN AN HOUR. AND SO IT DID WITH THE PEQUOD.

THE SAILS WERE TORN, THE SMALLER MASTS BROKEN, THE CREW ALL BUT WASHED FROM THE PLUNGING SHIP.

after EVERS

30

THE TIPS OF THE THREE MAIN MASTS GLOWED WITH AN UNEARTHLY PALLOR--

--AS DID AHAB'S HARPOON, WHICH HE BRANDISHED FIERCELY, KEEPING THE MEN FROM TURNING THE SHIP ABOUT.

STARBUCK URGED AHAB TO ORDER THE MAIN-TOP-SAIL STRUCK. "STRIKE NOTHING; LASH IT!" THE CAPTAIN ORDERED, SEEING THE STORM AS A NECESSARY MALADY, CARRYING US TO THE WHITE WHALE.

LASHING THE MAIN-TOP-SAIL HIGH ABOVE THE DECK, TASHTEGO CRIED OUT, "PLENTY TOO MUCH THUNDER UP HERE...WE DON'T WANT THUNDER; WE WANT RUM."

BELOWDECKS TO INFORM AHAB OF A CHANGE IN THE WEATHER, STARBUCK EYED THE MUSKET WITH WHICH AHAB ONCE THREATENED HIS LIFE...

...EYED IT--AND LEFT IT UNTOUCHED.

NOTHING NOW, NOT EVEN ENDING THE LIFE OF THE MADMAN AHAB HAD BECOME, COULD LIFT THE EVIL SPIRIT THAT HELD THE PEQUOD...

THE CARPENTER BEGAN MAKING THE NECESSARY CAULKING, CAUSING AHAB TO ACCUSE THE MAN OF BEING A SCAMP--

HE WANING WINDS OF THE STORM BROUGHT THE NEXT MORNING TO US, AND WITH E SUN RISING IN OUR WAKE-- N THOUGH THE HELMSMAN LED OUT OUR COURSE AS T-SOU'EAST" TO AHAB'S QUERY.

"YOU *LIE!*" SCREAMED AHAB, KNOCKING THE MAN TO THE GROUND-- ONLY TO FIND THE COMPASS NEEDLE, DEMAGNETIZED BY THE STORM, READING AS THE HELMSMAN HAD SAID.

3Y ACTING THE PART OF SORCERER AS HE FASHIONED A NEW NEEDLE FOR THE COMPASS, AHAB PROCEEDED TO PLAY ON THE CREW'S IGNORANCE AND SUPERSTITION, CALLING HIMSELF, "LORD OF THE LODESTONE."

--MAKING LEGS ONE DAY AND COFFINS THE NEXT.

TO DO SUCH A THING, SAID AHAB, WAS, "AS UNPRINCIPLED AS THE GODS."

ANOTHER MORNING CAME, THIS ONE BRINGING THE CRIES OF SEALS--A BAD OMEN QUICKLY FULFILLED BY A SEAMAN PLUNGING FROM THE MAINMAST INTO THE SEA. THE PEQUOD'S ROTTED LIFE-BUOY SUNK RATHER THAN SAVE THE DOOMED MAN, PROMPTING QUEEQUEG TO SUGGEST THAT HIS COFFIN WOULD MAKE AN EXCELLENT LIFE-BUOY.

"I DO NOT MEAN ANYTHING, SIR," THE CARPENTER REPLIED. "I DO AS I DO."

"THE GODS AGAIN," AHAB RETORTED.

AHAB LEANED OVER THE PEQUOD'S SIDE, STARING DOWN INTO THE SEA, A TEAR FALLING INTO THE WATER...

SEEING THE OLD MAN'S PENSIVENESS, STARBUCK JOINED HIM--AND AHAB BEGAN TO TALK OF HIS FORTY LONG YEARS ON THE SEA, FORTY YEARS OF TOIL AND PRIVATION. HE TALKED OF THE WIFE HE LOVED, SEEN BUT TWICE IN ALL THOSE YEARS...

"I FEEL DEADLY FAINT," HE ADMITTED, "BOWED AND HUMPED, AS THOUGH I WERE ADAM, STAGGERING BENEATH THE PILED CENTURIES SINCE PARADISE."

STARBUCK PLEADED WITH AHAB TO TURN BACK, TO END HIS VENGEFUL MISSION. BUT AHAB COULD NOT...

"WHAT IS IT--WHAT NAMELESS, INSCRUTABLE, UNEARTHLY THING IS IT; WHAT COZENING HIDDEN LORD AND MASTER, AND CRUEL, REMORSELESS EMPEROR COMMANDS ME;" AHAB WONDERED, "THAT AGAINST ALL NATURAL LOVINGS AND LONGINGS, I SO KEEP PUSHING AND CROWDING AND JAMMING MYSELF ON ALL THE TIME; RECKLESSLY MAKING ME READY TO DO WHAT IN MY OWN PROPER, NATURAL HEART, I DURST NOT SO MUCH AS DARE."

THEY COULD NOT TURN BACK, AHAB TOLD STARBUCK. "BY HEAVEN, MAN, WE ARE TURNED ROUND AND ROUND IN THIS WORLD, LIKE YONDER WINDLASS, AND FATE IS THE HANDSPIKE."

34

THE FIRST DAY OF THE CHASE HAD ARRIVED...

THERE SHE BLOWS!.. THERE SHE BLOWS! A HUMP LIKE A SNOW-HILL! IT IS *MOBY DICK!*

35

THE BOATS WERE PUT OVER AND THE MEN PADDLED SILENTLY AFTER THE GREAT WHALE--WHO SWAM WITH A GENTLE JOYOUSNESS AND A MIGHTY MILDNESS OF REPOSE IN SWIFTNESS.

THE BOATS WERE ALMOST UPON MOBY DICK WHEN HE SOUNDED, DIVING DEEP. "AN HOUR," PREDICTED AHAB...

...BUT IMMEDIATELY, SEA BIRDS BEGAN CIRCLING NEAR AHAB'S BOAT, A SIGN THAT A WHALE WAS NEAR. LEANING OVER THE SIDE, AHAB PEERED INTO THE DEPTHS--

--AND SAW THE IMMENSE, OPEN JAW OF THE WHITE WHALE RISING TOWARD HIM!

THE MEN WHIRLED THE BOAT ABOUT, BUT MOBY DICK TWISTED UNDER THE WATER, GRIPPING THE BOAT GENTLY IN THE SCROLL OF HIS JAW--

--AND THEN CRUNCHED THE BOAT IN HALF, DUMPING THE CREW IN THE SEA BEFORE SWIMMING OFF.

37

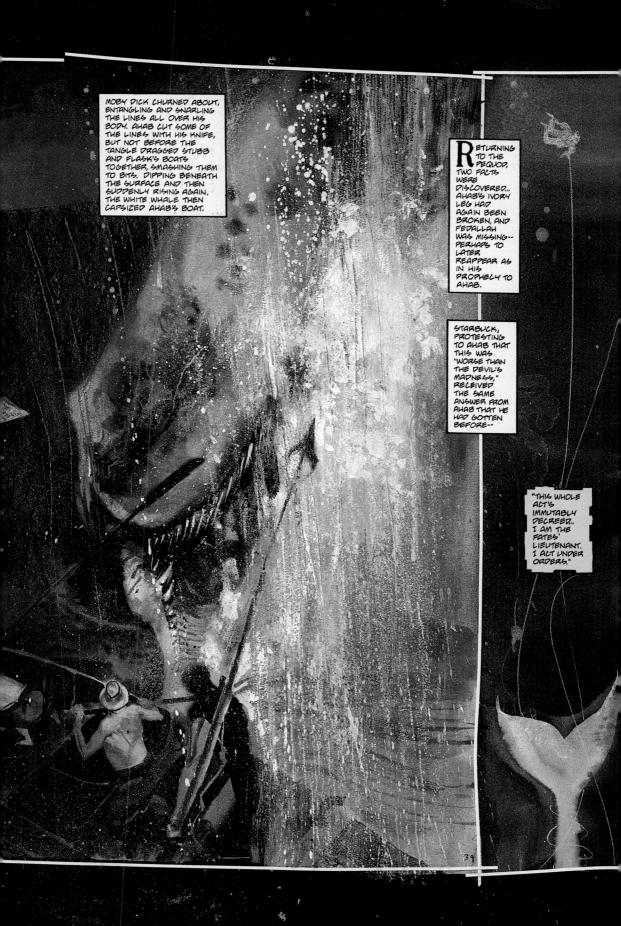

MOBY DICK CHURNED ABOUT, ENTANGLING AND SNARLING THE LINES ALL OVER HIS BODY. AHAB CUT SOME OF THE LINES WITH HIS KNIFE, BUT NOT BEFORE THE TANGLE DRAGGED STUBB AND FLASK'S BOATS TOGETHER, SMASHING THEM TO BITS. DIPPING BENEATH THE SURFACE AND THEN SUDDENLY RISING AGAIN, THE WHITE WHALE THEN CAPSIZED AHAB'S BOAT.

RETURNING TO THE PEQUOD, TWO FACTS WERE DISCOVERED... AHAB'S IVORY LEG HAD AGAIN BEEN BROKEN, AND FEDALLAH WAS MISSING-- PERHAPS TO LATER REAPPEAR AS IN HIS PROPHECY TO AHAB.

STARBUCK, PROTESTING TO AHAB THAT THIS WAS "WORSE THAN THE DEVIL'S MADNESS," RECEIVED THE SAME ANSWER FROM AHAB THAT HE HAD GOTTEN BEFORE--

"THIS WHOLE ACT'S IMMUTABLY DECREED... I AM THE FATES' LIEUTENANT. I ACT UNDER ORDERS."

39

THE THIRD DAY OF THE CHASE.

IN A MAD GESTURE, THE WHALE ROSE HIGH OUT OF THE WATER. THERE, ON HIS SIDE IN THE TANGLED HARPOON ROPES, WAS FEDALLAH--ANOTHER OMEN FULFILLED, THE FIRST HEARSE, NOT MADE BY HUMAN HANDS.

POINTING HIS MASSIVE FOREHEAD AT THE PEQUOD, MOBY DICK RUSHED AT THE SHIP, STAVING IN ITS FORWARD BOW--IT WAS THE SECOND PROPHECY, THE PEQUOD BECOMING A HEARSE MADE OF AMERICAN WOOD.

40

ENRAGED, AHAB DARTED HIS HARPOON INTO HIS NEMESIS, HIS PASSION ERUPTING...

"TO THE LAST I *GRAPPLE* WITH THEE; FROM HELL'S HEART I *STAB* AT THEE; FOR *HATE'S* SAKE I SPIT MY *LAST BREATH* AT THEE!"

BUT AS AHAB STOOPED TO CLEAR A SNARL IN THE LINE, IT LOOPED AROUND HIS NECK AND SNAPPED HIM OUT OF THE BOAT. "HEMP ONLY CAN KILL THEE...," THE THIRD PROPHECY HAD COME TO PASS.

AS THE PEQUOD SANK OUT OF SIGHT, TASHTEGO'S ARM PINNED A SKY-HAWK AGAINST THE TOP OF THE MAINMAST. THE SHIP, LIKE SATAN, WOULD NOT SINK TO HELL UNTIL SHE HAD CARRIED A PART OF THE LIVING HEAVEN WITH HER.

41

THE SINKING
SHIP CREATED
A GREAT
WHIRLPOOL WHICH
PULLED DOWN
ALMOST EVERYTHING
WITH IT. THE VORTEX
DID FINALLY SETTLE,
AND WHEN IT DID
THE GREAT WHITE
SHROUD OF THE SEA
ROLLED ON AS IT
ROLLED FIVE
THOUSAND YEARS
AGO...

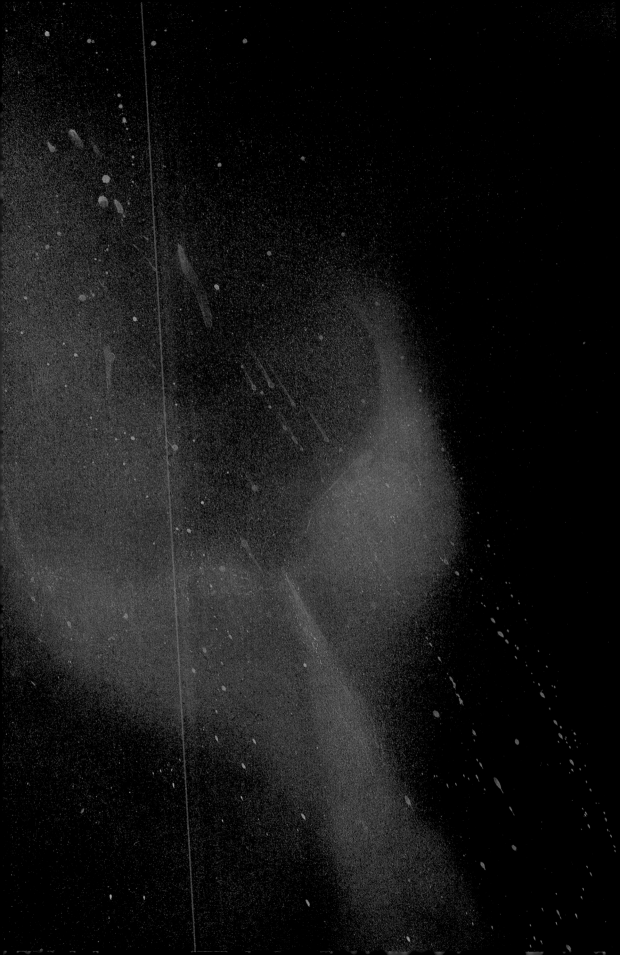

THE DRAMA'S DONE. WHY THEN DOES ANY ONE STEP FORTH?--BECAUSE ONE DID SURVIVE THE WRECK.

BUOYED UP BY THE COFFIN, FOR ALMOST ONE WHOLE DAY AND NIGHT, I FLOATED ON A SOFT AND DIRGE-LIKE MAIN. ON THE SECOND DAY, A SAIL DREW NEAR, AND PICKED ME UP AT LAST. IT WAS THE RACHEL, THAT IN HER RETRACING SEARCH AFTER HER MISSING CHILDREN, ONLY FOUND ANOTHER ORPHAN.

HERMAN MELVILLE was born in New York on August 1, 1819, one of eight offspring of a well-to-do merchant and his wife. When Melville was 12, his father died, leaving the family virtually penniless. Melville's schooling ended when he was 15 and he took a series of jobs, working briefly as a bank clerk, sales clerk, farmer and teacher. At the age of 18, Melville shipped as a cabin boy to Liverpool; this first voyage instilled in him a lifetime love for the sea and sailing. Upon his return, Melville taught school in upstate New York, before shipping at 21 for the South Seas aboard a whaling ship, an adventure that inspired *Moby Dick.* After 18 months, disenchanted with the tyrannical captain, Melville deserted the ship at the Marquesas Islands and was captured by cannibals, an ordeal from which he later fashioned *Typee* and *Mardi.* Rescued after four months by an Australian ship, Melville traveled to Tahiti, where he worked as a field laborer and researched the island life later depicted in *Omoo.* He shipped from Tahiti in 1843 on a whaler, departing at Hawaii to enlist as a seaman on a Navy man-of-war; Melville's life aboard the frigate served as the basis for *White-Jacket.* When he was discharged in 1844, Melville returned home and began to craft fiction from his experiences. His first five books — the exotic adventure stories *Typee* (1846), *Omoo* (1847), *Mardi* (1849), *Redburn* (1849) and *White-Jacket* (1850) — quickly won Melville fame and a wide following. In 1850, Melville and his wife, whom he had married in 1847, moved to Massachusetts, where he formed a strong friendship with Nathaniel Hawthorne. Melville's popularity began to wane with the publication of the epic *Moby Dick* (1851). Although he continued to publish novels, short stories and poems until his death, Melville never regained literary success. From 1857 until 1860, he tried unsuccessfully to make a living as a lecturer. Impoverished, Melville moved to New York, where, in 1866, he gained appointment as a customs inspector, a job he was to hold for 19 years. Melville's last years were spent in obscurity, and his death on September 28, 1891, passed unnoticed. A reappraisal by literary scholars thirty years later restored Melville's reputation as a great literary figure. His last work, *Billy Budd,* completed just before his death, was finally published in 1924.

BILL SIENKIEWICZ was born in 1958 in Pennsylvania and grew up in New Jersey. After attending the Newark School of Fine and Industrial Art, he began illustrating comic books in 1978. Sienkiewicz's credits include *Fantastic Four, Elektra: Assassin, Moon Knight, New Mutants, Shadow, Stray Toasters* and *Brought to Light.* His individualistic, highly stylized art has won Sienkiewicz much acclamation, including the 1987 Jack Kirby Award for best artist, five Certificates of Merit from the Society of Illustrators, Italy's 1986 Yellow Kid and Gran Guinigi Awards, and Spain's 1988 Medallion de Aple d'Huez Award. A noted magazine and record album designer and illustrator, Sienkiewicz also is working on a pilot program for a MTV animated series.

D.G. CHICHESTER was born in Connecticut in 1964, and graduated from New York University with a degree in film. He was an editor for Marvel Comics' Epic line, where he worked on such titles as *Marshal Law, Groo the Wanderer, Stray Toasters* and *Hellraiser.* Chichester has written a number of comic books, including *Shield,* and co-wrote *St. George, Powerline, Doctor Zero* and *Critical Mass.* In addition to his work in the comics field, he is writing several screenplays.

A

CLASSIC OFFER FROM THE PUBLISHERS OF CLASSICS ILLUSTRATED®

THE ULTIMATE SAMURAI ADVENTURE!

The first English edition of the legendary black and white Japanese series that set the standard for the samurai graphic story genre.

Over six million Japanese comics fans read **LONE WOLF and CUB**. Find out why.

New cover illustrations by DARK KNIGHT artist **Frank Miller** and MOBY DICK artist **Bill Sienkiewicz.**

Lone Wolf and Cub is a sophisticated epic of Japan's violent past. Some issues contain extreme violence and sexual situations. Reader discretion is advised.

Please send me the following issues of **Lone Wolf and Cub**. I have checked my selections below, and have added 75¢ per title U.S. ($1.50 per title Canadian) for postage and handling (Chicago residents must add 8% sales tax). I have enclosed my check or money order in U.S. funds for $_____. Offer Expires April 30, 1990.

Lone Wolf and Cub #1: $2.95 ($3.75 Canada) Bonus premiere issue — 96 pages

	U.S./CAN		U.S./CAN		U.S./CAN		U.S./CAN
#2: $1.95/2.60		#8: $2.50/3.25		#14: $2.50/3.25		#20: $2.50/3.25
#3: $1.95/2.60		#9: $2.50/3.25		#15: $2.50/3.25		#21: $2.50/3.2
#4: $1.95/2.60		#10: $2.50/3.25		#16: $2.50/3.25		#22: $2.50/3.2
#5: $1.95/2.60		#11: $2.50/3.25		#17: $2.50/3.25		#23: $2.50/3.2
#6: $1.95/2.60		#12: $2.50/3.25		#18: $2.50/3.25		#24: $2.50/3.2
#7: $1.95/2.60		#13: $2.50/3.25		#19: $2.50/3.25		#25: $2.50/3.2

No foreign orders. Allow 6-8 weeks for delivery. Please make checks payable to First Publishing, In

Name _____ Address _____

City _____ State _____ Zip _____

Mail to: Lone Wolf and Cub Dept. MD   435 North LaShalle Street   Chicago, IL 60